Good Moves

Seven Questions for Clergy to Ask Upon Leaving and Entering Positions of Leadership

A Systems Perspective

by

Phillip S. Washburn

Strategic Book Publishing and Rights Co.

Strategic Book Publishing and Rights Co.
12620 FM 1960, Suite A4-507
Houston TX 77065
www.sbpra.com

ISBN: 978-1-61897-981-0

Contents

Introduction   v

Chapter One: The Ecclesiastical Dating Game:

     Searching for a Match   1

       Relational Rupture   6

       Cutoff   10

       Shrouded in Mystery   12

       Not Letting Go   13

Chapter Two: Leaving Well:

     The Connected Disconnect   15

       Some Advice for Clergy: Five Do's   16

       One Don't   18

       Some Advice for Congregations   19

       Going Out the Door with Grace   20

Chapter Three: Contemplating the New Position:

     A New Opportunity to Define a Self   22

       What is Self-differentiation?   24

       Transition as a Time to Focus

         on Self-differentiation   32

Chapter Four: Entering a New Field of Anxiety:

The Congregation that Awaits   35

Four Examples of Highly Anxious

Congregational Behavior   36

Chapter Five: Seven Questions for Managing

One's Own Anxiety Upon Entering

the Congregation that Awaits   45

Question area #1:

Dealing with Embitterment   46

Question area #2:

Dealing with the Past Recycled   47

Question area #3:

Dealing with Misplaced Expectations 49

Question area #4:

Dealing with Unresolved Pain   50

Question area #5:

Dealing with Secrets   51

Question area #6:

Dealing with Weak Leadership   53

Question area #7:

Dealing with Under-and

Over-functioning   55

Chapter Six: Summing Up   59

Notes   63

Bibliography for Further Reading   67

Introduction

More clergy are moving more often these days. Increasingly anxious congregations (often rent by internal divisions) are receiving and losing (or dismissing) their clergy with greater frequency. There is a way in which the overload of expectations that couples bring to their marriages in today's culture resemble the overload of expectations that churches and clergy bring to their "marriages." In both arenas the "couples" (marital and ecclesiastical), upon failing to find their longed-for fulfillment in each other, separate and move on, sometimes amicably, mostly not. Whatever the reasons, the rate of marital divorce is higher; the length of clergy tenure is shorter.

Shorter clergy tenure only compounds an anxiety already rife in congregations. If, indeed, the level of anxiety in congregations reflects a generally higher level of anxiety in the culture at large, then increased clergy movement further raises anxiety in both the congregations they serve and in themselves.

For clergy, moving from one congregation to another is, under the best of circumstances, inherently stressful. There is the stress of grief (engaged or denied in varying degrees) involved in departing a congregation, even when the feelings are mixed—perhaps especially when mixed. If the clergy person is partnered/married, there is the stress of uprooting a partner/spouse and often children as well. Grief, loss, and resentment—the "big three" of transitional dynamics—have a way of ricocheting back to the clergy person. And then, of course, there is the stress of entering a new and by definition quasi-mysterious setting with its unlimited potential for blind-siding a newly arrived "reverend." As mentioned, these stressors exist even in the best of circumstances. In highly anxious times they are made worse and can overwhelm.

Clergy contemplating or facing a move (voluntarily or not) face three "how to" issues: first, how to assess a potential new congregation to which they feel called; second, how to disengage from their current position once a new position has been obtained; third, how to engage the new setting. A signal means for negotiating these "how-to's" and for managing anxiety in the process is the application of a way of thinking derived from a systems perspective, that is, from the increasingly well-known natural systems theory of Murray Bowen as applied by Rabbi Edwin Friedman specifically to clergy and congregations. Those inclined to delve more deeply into systems thinking may want to refer to the bibliography at the end of this monograph. The thinking here represented, however, is my own application of a perspective that is helping more and more clergy negotiate what could be termed "white water ministry." (A river swiftly flowing over rocks kicks up a white froth emblematic of its destructive power, a boater-beware warning to those who dare to ride its dangerous currents.) Ministry today might, metaphorically speaking, be likened to rafting down a river of roiling rapids over which there can be little or no control.

There is, however, one area over which clergy may exert a measure of control, and that is over their own reactivity, or more accurately over the management of themselves. The thrust of what follows is an invitation to clergy to comport themselves as non-anxious presences—or, if not entirely non-anxious, at least less-anxious presences—with some tips as how that may be done as they transition from one invariably anxious congregational system to another.

For clergy, transitions begin when they contemplate a move, when they begin to look "out there" for a new congregational partner. The clergy person's search is matched by a congregation's search. When they find each other, the "mating game" begins with each side attempting to discern if they are a "match." It is inevitably assumed that what makes for a good match are the compatibility factors, such as whether they think alike, share the same outlook and tastes, etc. What is seldom recognized is that the more crucial element in how the partners in a new clergy/congregational marriage will bond has less to do with their presumptive compatibility and more to do with how each has disengaged from its previous relationship. As with serial marriage, no matter how compatible the partners, unresolved issues have an uncanny way of traveling whole into the next marriage, often explosively.

Given this reality, it behooves both clergy and congregations to disengage well; that is, to give the process of separation the time it deserves and to honor their time together, even if that time has had its difficulties. Leaving is often, if not always, fraught with issues of abandonment and rejection. The wounds that all too often accompany departure are slow to heal. The carryover of open wounds can easily infect the next pastorate.

For clergy, using the time of transition—by definition a time of high anxiety—to focus on their own functioning, on what they wish to be about, on self-definition, on what they will and will not respond to rather than on what others may be demanding, can be a means to managing their own anxiety. There is no little pressure on clergy to give up self to please congregants, to avoid taking clear positions. The dependence on approval from others is endemic to the position of clergy. It is a formidable task not to cede self to "the group" that pays one's salary and throws up an infinite array of needs to be met on demand. But this very reality is all the more reason for clergy to take responsibility for how they function.

As clergy enter a new situation, a situation almost inevitably fraught with anxiety, the inclination to please (almost irresistible) can turn them into depositories for the content of the congregations' anxiety. Rampant anxiety undermines both personal and congregational health, which is why it is crucial that clergy find ways of lowering the level of anxiety, first in themselves and then, to the extent they can function as a non-anxious (or at least less anxious) presence, in the congregation. Functioning non-anxiously doesn't mean one is free of anxiety. It means learning how to function less reactively despite the discomfort of one's own anxiety.

To this end, chapter five offers seven questions (or areas of disarming inquiry) designed to assist clergy in managing their own anxiety as they enter a new setting. The questions are designed to help clergy manage their own reactivity to the confrontational reactivity they may encounter in their new setting.

Transitions, by nature, are not easy. This small volume is intended as a resource for making the stress-laden transitions between congregations less harrowing for clergy and even, upon occasion, more satisfyingly creative.

This monograph is, admittedly, over-full of advice. Murray Bowen urged the systems therapists he trained to "never give advice," which is, of course, a form of advice. But he was right. Advice-giving is largely ineffective. If it were effective, advisees would slap their foreheads and ask, "Why didn't I think of that?" whereupon their functioning would instantly improve. For some reason it doesn't happen that way.

Chapter 2 elucidates what I count as good advice when leaving a congregation. I confess, however, that I wish I'd thought to do half of what I've written about in that chapter when I was in the process of disengaging from my various pastorates. And I wish I'd had at tongue-tip even some of the seven questions cited in Chapter 5 when negotiating my transitions between calls. I didn't. But they are offered, as is this short book, in the hope that the thinking will be of use to others in managing themselves in the midst of negotiating the rapids of what I have termed above a "white water ministry."

Phil Washburn
May 2012

Chapter One

The Ecclesiastical Dating Game: Searching for a Match

After ten satisfying years serving a small but warm and responsive congregation, the thought began to press in upon a pastor now in her mid-thirties that perhaps she ought to consider a move. She didn't really want to consider it. She knew and liked the congregation; the congregation knew and liked, indeed, loved her. It was, one might say, a comfortable "ecclesiastical marriage." But it was, she had begun to think, rather too comfortable. She could stay, she realized, for "the duration," but if she did stay, how would she know what she was made of. Unless she undertook a more challenging and most likely less comfortable position elsewhere, she would never know.

This unsettling thought had been moving to the forefront of her mind for some months, until finally she worked up her profile and began "the search." It was not easy to bring herself to this point, for in the very act of making her profile available she had begun, however subtly, to unmoor herself emotionally from a place to which she was deeply attached.

Nonetheless, she knew it was something she had to do. (See notes, chapter one, #1)

And so it is that even for clergy enjoying relatively long-term and satisfying pastorates, there comes a day they begin to ask themselves:

- When is it time to go?
- When does a congregation need new leadership?
- When do I need to revitalize myself by tackling a new set of problems/issues?
- Will I lose my edge if I stay put?
- At what point do I risk being too old to be "marketable" to a new congregation?

From the other side, prospective congregations may wonder:

- Does this candidate lack ambition or energy having stayed put for so long?
- Has her/his welcome been over-stayed?
- Has something finally gone sour?

Conversely, other questions abound about clergy unhappily enduring short-term pastorates, who are seeking, perhaps desperately, a way out. Of these clergy congregations may ask, or at least wonder:

- Why are they looking so soon?
- Have they a short-term track record?

- What's that about?
- Perhaps they have too much edge!
- If they are disgruntled in their current situation, will they bring their disgruntlement with them?

Either way, clergy attempting to leave long or short-term tenures, happy or "un," will at some point go a-courtin'. As anyone who has dated around knows, it can be a tricky process. Each potential partner, in sidling up to the other, will put his or her best foot forward, while each will be fishing simultaneously to find the other's other foot—the other's not-best-foot. Conversely, they may not want to notice the other's not-best-foot; they may simply want to fall blindly in love. In any event, each will pose questions to the other. It can all take on the characteristics of Match.Com, and not necessarily to good effect.

The questions posed by Match.Com are designed to determine compatibility. Do prospective couples have similar tastes in music and movies? Do they jive with each other when it comes to recreation and travel? The courtship between congregations and clergy often poses similar compatibility questions.

A congregation, for its part, will attempt to determine the compatibility of a potential candidate's theological orientation: such as how the candidate handles scripture (more literally or more metaphorically); how social justice issues, and which issues, figure into the candidates preaching; how "spiritual" the candidate is; whether the candidate's leadership style is folksy and intimate or more formal and distant; how the candidate leans with respect to services that are child-friendly versus those designed for adults only.

The natural tendency is to find a likely match by determining compatibility, the back side of which is to screen for incompatibility. *Must Love Dogs*, as the movie of that title put it, announces that for any on-line dating candidate to hate dogs would be a deal breaker. But the requirement to love dogs is a dubious mating filter. There are, after all, psychotic dog lovers. In fact, someone who is "dog neutral" might make a marvelous mate.

In any event, clergy, for their part, do much the same screening. In approaching a potential position, they, too, do their best to determine how compatible the match might be by assessing the congregation's theological orientation: how the authority of the Bible is regarded; which social justice issues are embraced and which avoided; what is the preferred worship style, the congregation's receptivity to children in services, and so on. On both sides there are "must love dogs" filters—screening components for sifting the possibilities, and impossibilities.

Determining the "compatibility level" is obviously important. A social justice left-leaning activist clergy person will not likely last in a politically conservative, right-leaning traditionalist congregation. But there is a crucial factor, unrelated to compatibility, which matters just as much, if not more than apparent compatibility. When it comes to assessing how well a new relationship (i.e., the next clergy tenure) may fare, the manner in which the previous relationship was disengaged from is of critical importance. This applies to both the congregation and the clergy candidate. With respect to the congregation, specifically, under what circumstances did the previous minister leave? Or the previous several ministers? What was the character of the departure? With respect to the clergy, what were the circumstances of his or her leaving the last position? Or the last several positions? What was the character of his or her departure? (See notes, chapter one, #2)

A congregational setting that bodes well for the next pastor is one in which, upon the departure of the previous pastor there was a healthy celebration of that pastor's tenure mixed, appropriately enough, with sorrow at its ending. The emotional connection between the congregation and its pastor is positive, but can be moved on from. Pastor and congregation are able to say "goodbye." The same holds true of a clergy candidate, i.e., the connection with the previous congregation was positive, but can be moved on from.

The kind of departures from which both pastor and congregation have more difficulty moving on are those in which there are unresolved emotional intensities. Unresolved emotional intensity means, in effect, that former relationships are still hot-wired, still obsess the partners. Even though they've moved out, so to speak, they haven't been able to move on. Unresolved emotional intensities take a variety of forms. Four of the more common of them are as follows:

1. A leaving due to a relational rupture, fraught with factional disputes, more like an angry divorce.
2. A leaving that is a blatant cutoff, a disappearance without so much as a goodbye, with nothing processed.
3. A leaving shrouded in mystery, often generating secrets and gossip. No one knows exactly why the departure/separation occurred.
4. A leaving that has, in effect, never really happened. The congregation is emotionally unable to let go of the "perfect pastor."

Relational Rupture

Perhaps the most common form of unresolved emotional intensity is that of the relational rupture. Relational ruptures can take an almost infinite variety of forms. Here's one:

A prosperous suburban church brought on board a new female Associate Minister to whom was assigned nearly all of the pastoral responsibility. The male Senior Minister retained most of the preaching responsibilities, the greater share of civic and interfaith involvements, and the entire fund raising role. The arrangement was initially agreeable all around. Before long, however, the Senior and the Associate developed an intense dislike of each other. Staff meetings became distressing exercises in mutual sabotage and acrimony, to the staff's considerable discomfort—an emotional state that soon leaked out to the congregation-at-large, which, ostrich-like, tried to remain in denial. The toxic inability of these two to work together became undeniable, however, when the Senior Minister demanded that the Associate be terminated. Denominational mediators were brought in, but to no avail. Finally the governing board agreed to the Senior's demand, but did an about-face when some in the congregation rose in defense of the Associate, whose pastoral attentions had created an aggrieved, voluble, and not inconsiderable constituency (not to mention the gender issues that surfaced). With the fissures in the congregation rapidly growing wider, the governing board, fearing that the church's survival was at stake, decided to clean house. The entire clergy staff was terminated, including three others beyond the Senior and Associate.

In the aftermath, no resolution of the conflict between the Senior and Associate came about, nor between factions within the congregation which had taken sides. The lay leadership's mantra was that everything would straighten out as soon as a new Senior Minister could be called; to wit, the interim period was foreshortened. When the new Senior Minister arrived, this time a woman, not surprisingly the old difficulties recycled. Subsequent Associate Ministers had to be "let go" and conflict emerged between the Senior and the by-then powerful Minister of Music (who had "helpfully" filled the power vacuum during the interim period). The board attempted to monitor, even control, its clergy staff, an impingement that frustrated their functioning and did nothing to prevent interpersonal conflicts from arising. Ongoing resentments continued to fester, inhibiting decision making. The congregation remained stuck. When, some five years on, the relatively new and by now unhappy Senior Minister left for another post, the church went through three Interim Ministers who either resigned in disgruntlement or were fired.

The ongoing disarray in the life of this congregation was due largely to the fact that none of the original factional polarities had been addressed. (Some sided with the Associate, some with the Senior, some were fed up with both.) No effort was made by clergy or board members to hear what the congregants were feeling, seeing, and thinking, much less to process their grief. The leave-taking of the staff dealt with nothing that had happened. The constituencies on all sides were disconsolate. The predictable result was that the emotional intensities never cooled, but rather continued to erupt volcanically in the subsequent clergy tenures.

The grief that arose from this unprocessed rupture resurfaced as bitterness (a distortion of grief). The bitterness was unleashed on those who followed, sabotaging the "once-and-future-clergy" including the interims.

It would have helped, and possibly avoided the ongoing morass of recrimination, had there been an effort to hear what needed to be heard, and then shared what was heard, had the emotional topography of the congregation been shared as candidly and neutrally as possible. Congregants needed to know that their opinions counted. Glossing over the dissonance did not well serve the community.

It should be noted that the candidates who interviewed for the position of Senior Minister were told of the church's entire staff having been fired. (Most search committees, in what is offered up as virtuous transparency, will usually candidly inform clergy candidates of the congregation's most recent difficulties.) With this fact admitted, however, the search committee emphasized that the search now was for someone who would unite the congregation. The disagreeable past was to be dropped as soon as possible. The right successor, each candidate was told (if not explicitly, then implicitly) would doubtless help them do that by proving to be far superior to their immediate predecessor. This type of appeal to become a rescuer, a "savior" is seductive. It invites a kind of collusion to come together in a shared distaste-come-disgust over the immediate past. (Courtship candor is often more self-and-other deceptive than is generally recognized.)

In any event, what was not being addressed was that the break with the past had been too abrupt, not to mention the fact that no effort had gone into working through the still festering ruptures. What was not understood in the interview process by either church or clergy was that the capacity of their potential "marriage" to thrive had less to do with what they held in common (theological outlook, taste in sacred music, and such) than with how they each had left their previous relationships. In the case of the church, it had been badly, which bode ill for any future relationship. Unresolved emotional intensity thereby got passed on down through the generations.

Cutoff

A second form of unresolved emotional intensity arises from cutoff. Cutoffs occur in relationships that become so conflicted that the partners refuse to have anything more to do with each other. This happens in families, of course. Aunt Georgina has refused for years to speak with Aunt Matilda. No one knows why, but family gatherings cannot include both at the same time. Cutoffs tend to persist in families down through the generations. One side of the family has little or nothing to do with the other side. Again, no one quite knows why. No one knows when it began. No one talks about it. It just is.

Unresolved separation issues often perpetuate grief in the form of suspicion and fear. Some churches are birthed in cutoffs, that is to say they separated from an originating congregation, usually over some controversy. Long after the controversy is largely forgotten, the two congregations refuse to have anything to do with each other. The suspicion and fear live on. Each has "circled the wagons" in a defensive position. The unspoken insistence is that those inside must stick together against those outside. This generates a closeness, or fusion, among the "faithful" built on agreement along a required line of thinking. But it also makes for further ruptures within the circle with any who deviate from the "party line."

Just as churches can and do cut off from one another, so clergy sometimes cut off from their pastorates. The reasons are as diverse as the clergy themselves. Two instances by way of examples will suffice.

In the first, a pastor became increasingly disgruntled, but could not bring herself to address her deepening discontent with the congregation through appropriate channels. The internal pressure built up until the "dam broke." She simply upped and left, announcing flatly that she was breaking their mutual agreement to finish out the three remaining years of her contracted tenure. She did not wish to stay and wasn't going to. There was nothing, she announced, that they could do about it.

In the second instance, a pastor who had become increasingly unavailable to his parishioners, finally, one day ran off with the former associate's ex-wife (who was still a member of the congregation), leaving both his own wife and the church behind, without an explanation, or even a "goodbye." The congregation was, of course, shocked and dismayed. But the lingering effect on the congregation was profound distrust, not only of clergy generally, but of itself. How had it been so completely blind-sided? Was its capacity for discernment deficient? The result was a near inability to risk choosing a successor candidate.

Shrouded in Mystery

A third form of unresolved emotional intensity arises in a church scene striated with secrets, often revolving around clergy behavior, or more likely misbehavior. If, for example, there has been unacknowledged clergy sexual misconduct, accompanied as is almost always the case by a below-ground flow of gossip, and if the misconduct remains unacknowledged even after the departure of the minister, so also the habit of secrecy remains. With secrets, the game is power. Some are in on it, others are not. Communication is frozen, or as Edwin Friedman once put it, "Secrets become plaque on the arteries of communication." Secrets make it extremely difficult for a congregation to know itself and, lacking self-knowledge, to deal effectively with its problems.

They lead to the death of trust, or, metaphorically speaking, to a kind of congregational heart-failure.

The main point is this: secrets prevent the dissipation of emotional intensity. Nothing surfaces to where it can be dealt with. Secrets create a condition that persists for generations. For some churches it is a way of being, and not a pleasant one.

Not Letting Go

A fourth form of unresolved emotional intensity is that of not letting go. Usually this has to do with a much-loved former pastor, though it could have to do with a much-detested former pastor as well. A much-loved pastor can become not only a hard act to follow, but something of an idol of the past, from whom the congregation cannot emotionally detach and against whom no present or future clergy can ever measure up. Persistent emotional fusion can keep a congregation stuck for years and make mincemeat of the idol's successors. Genuine grieving at the departure of a much loved clergy person is one thing; permanent grief borne of permanent emotional attachment is another. Though the clergy person has left (or "departed"), in fact he/she is still ghost-like, oppressively present.

This can be a difficult condition for a prospective successor to discern, as the immediate aftermath of grief surrounding the departure of the previous pastor may seem quite healthy. It can be too early to tell whether or not the church will be able in due time to let go. One means of discernment is to try to determine just how dependent the former minister may still be on the adulation of the congregation. What kind of connectedness is being maintained? Some ongoing connectedness is desirable and healthy. Nonetheless, has the pastor moved on? If so, the congregation will likely do so as well.

These four instances of unresolved emotional intensity have more to do with how the incoming clergy relationship will "take" than do most of the compatibility factors that preoccupy most ecclesiastical courtships. The next chapter will attempt to describe ways to avoid, or at least minimize the problems that come with leaving.

Chapter Two

Leaving Well:
The Connected Disconnect

The acceptance of a new "call" entails, obviously, leaving one's current pastoral position. If the premise of chapter one is on target, then leaving well impacts entering well; which is to say, leaving well helps, if not determines, how well the next relationship will bond.

So what might it mean to leave well? The truism is that good "goodbyes" are a prerequisite for good "hellos." There is much useful advice "out there" these days urging clergy to honor their departures, specifically not to rush out the door too quickly, to give adequate time to the disengagement process. The advice is commendable. But the often unanswered question is: What should be the goal of this time? What makes this time potentially valuable for both clergy and congregations to make an effective transition to their next "marriage?"

The answer lies in the way the connections of the closing tenure are honored. The ball for this is very much in the clergy's court. How clergy articulate their leaving and the reason for it is crucial.

Phillip S. Washburn
Some Advice for Clergy: Five Do's

One, the congregation's lay leadership deserves fair warning of what's about to become public. Aside from family and one's closest friends, they should be the first to know. (For Associate Ministers and/or other clergy staff positions, it may be most appropriate to begin with the accountability structure i.e., the Senior Minister and/or the appropriate personnel committee.) Do this, if at all possible, face to face. A face to face meeting entails answering the question "why?" The objective reason for leaving may be that of receiving a call from another congregation, being moved by the bishop, poor health, even leaving the ministry altogether, or retirement. No matter the reason, just below the surface there will inevitably lurk a mess of questions, many if not most of them not asked aloud. Could you, our clergy person, not have chosen to stay longer? What's the appeal of the other congregation whose call you've accepted, or the bishop's placement you've agreed to, or the alternative profession you've sought out, or the retirement into which you're so happily sailing off? Unless there is considerable relief at your going, the most common underlying question is, "What's wrong with us that you've chosen not to stay?" Issues of abandonment and rejection abound. Many, if not most in the congregation, feel they have a relationship with you—a personal one (however full of projections). What have these relationships meant to

16

you? It takes time to process even some of these questions. Give yourself the time. Leavings that are too abrupt short change the possibilities here.

A side note: It is not uncommon for clergy to duck these often awkward questions, spoken or unspoken, by falling back on "call" language, thereby triangulating God into the decision. Quite probably parishioners see through this "ducking."

Two, the letter of resignation to the congregation needs to address some of the personal concerns set forth in number one above. The congregation needs to know they matter to you. Tell them so.

Three, even if, as the clergy person, your time with this congregation has been mixed, even if you are ambivalent about your experience, the members are now part of your life-history, and you of theirs. Whenever and wherever possible, and especially from the pulpit, state what has been important and/or valuable to you about your time in this place, what you've learned, what you've struggled with, what you wish you'd been able to accomplish (rather than how you're disappointed with them!), what you might have done differently. Name and celebrate what together "we" have accomplished.

Four, review the road you've traveled together and state where you think things now stand. Articulate what you hope for this congregation as it makes its way into the future under new leadership. Lift up the congregation's strengths.

Five, take responsibility for your going (even if it has been imposed by a bishop— after all that's the ecclesiastical system you have chosen to work within). Be as transparent as you can be about your hopes for your own future.

All of these do's are about being as constructive as possible. They are about connecting past accomplishments with optimism about the future, while at the same time acknowledging that nothing lasts forever except effort and endeavor and the value of honesty with one another. It is difficult to say how long it may take to adequately process these do's, but surely it takes more than two or three weeks.

One Don't

Don't leave it a mystery as to what your leaving is about! If a congregation doesn't have some understanding of why you are leaving, they can and likely will interpret it as somehow their fault and subsequently get stuck in their own guilt and/or grief. Conversely, they may defensively project their own resentment and/or guilt by attempting to make it your fault, as in "You can't quit, you're fired. We never liked you anyway!"

In the end, individual clergy must find their way, given their specific temperament and situation, to disengage in the best way possible. But obviously, leaving well is not entirely up to the clergy person. The congregation has a role in this as well.

Some Advice for Congregations

There is a tendency for congregations, composed as they are of very human, human beings, to want to skirt the discomfort, the grief of separation. (Clergy, being very human, human beings, are not above skirting this either.) The congregation's mantra often becomes, "Let's get a new pastor in here as soon as possible." In an effort to avoid the discomfort of "goodbye," a congregation may want to focus its entire attention on what comes next. The leadership needs to short circuit this tendency.

Much the same list of do's and don'ts applies to congregations as to clergy. For example, not only must the pastor communicate with the congregation as a whole, but so must the lay leadership. It is for them to express appreciation for the ministry now ending. Even clergy tenures fraught with difficulties possess positive dimensions (though admittedly there are exceptions to this, clergy sexual predators being at or near the top of the list). The task for lay leadership is to articulate for the congregation the inherent sadness that attends the loss of the current pastoral presence. This can and should be elaborated upon during the allotted period between resignation and actual departure. The leadership needs to provide opportunities for members of the congregation to say what this ministry has meant to them, what has been valuable and what will be missed. It is important to mark and celebrate the time that is now ending. Most crucially, the lay leadership must lead the congregation in putting first things first: they must make clear that saying goodbye precedes focusing on the search (if that is the church's polity) for a new minister. The rule of thumb, as with most of life, should be to take one step at a time. (See notes, chapter 2, #1)

Going out the Door with Grace

In sum, the process of disengaging needs to be about the connections that have been made and their lasting value, perhaps leavened with an honest acknowledgement of where the struggles have been. A light touch helps with this. Departures often free up what may have been locked down by overly serious intensities accrued along the way. Long buried emotionally loaded subjects that could not be, or at least weren't, talked about may now bubble up. These "bubblings" can become opportunities for resolution.

In any event, congregations want and need the blessing of their pastors. Now is the time to confer it. It's good, too, if a congregation can find ways to confer its blessing on the departing pastor. Both clergy and congregants can probably use some healing, some resolution to whatever the conflicts may have been (and it's unimaginable that there weren't some).

Increasingly these days there are liturgies for both clergy and lay members who are departing a congregation. These can be tailored to meet each specific context and are well worth making part of the process of leaving.

Chapter Three

Contemplating the New Position:
A New Opportunity to Define a Self

To accept a new position in a new place is, obviously, to agree to enter, as we say, "God knows what!" It is to enter the unknown, an unfamiliar setting in which just how a new set of relationships will play out is anybody's guess. It is to enter the unknown. No matter how savvy the clergy person, there will be aspects in the new setting about which he/she will be clueless. It can't be helped.

Clergy, upon entering a new situation (even those with prophetic predispositions) will want to be accepted, better yet appreciated, by their congregations. They will want their prospective ministry to flourish. To this end, they will try, naturally enough, to please their new employers. But herein lies a trap. In order to please a congregation, clergy, to one degree or another, tend to give up "self."

Marriage is perhaps the prime arena in which the difficulty of retaining self is posed. When two people marry they become, as the service may say, "one." What the service doesn't say is, *which one*. (See notes, chapter 3, #1)

The tendency in marriage is for one partner to absorb self from the other, who correspondingly cedes self to the other. (A self that absorbs self, no less than a self that cedes self, actually lacks self. If it didn't, it wouldn't need to borrow self from others.) The underlying issue is how to marry yet retain a sense of self. Well differentiated partners neither absorb nor cede selves. In reality, however, there are relatively few well differentiated partners! Indeed, the axiom is, no one is ever completely differentiated.

Clergy/congregation marriages are not dissimilar. The pressure on clergy to give up self in order to please their congregants can be enormous. There are spoken and unspoken demands on the part of congregations to deliver what is wanted, which is much for many. Clergy are asked to be all things to all people. Aside from being a recipe for burnout, the demands themselves, in their multiplicity, are inevitably contradictory. To please some is often to annoy others, or worse, to arouse enmity.

What does it look like when clergy "give up self?" They avoid positions or stands that displease. They adopt a persona that adapts as adroitly as possible to what is wanted. They yield to group-think. They agree when they don't, really. Clarity is ducked. Personal convictions are camouflaged or jettisoned altogether. What is presented publicly is a pseudo self.

Whether or not some yielding of self is unavoidable in ministry (there being no such thing as 100% differentiation), the "yielding" runs into the reality that, no matter how much self clergy give up, it is never enough. The effort to please never ultimately pleases. Clergy often end up like gerbils on a treadmill—never getting anywhere while exhausting themselves in the process.

But in the midst of a transition there lies a golden opportunity. When clergy prepare to move to a new position, their anxiety level almost certainly rises. Along with it, the desire to please rises as well. If, however, in the midst of this anxiety one keeps in mind that pleasing others is an unsatisfactory and often ineffective form of ministry, not to mention a wearying emotional drain, then a transitional time provides the time and space to step back and consider what it might take not to yield up self, or at least to yield up less of it, in the setting to which one is headed. The key to what it takes is something called "self-differentiation."

What Is Self-differentiation?

To get at what differentiation is, it is useful to start with its opposite: fusion. In families that are fused, individual independence is frowned upon, or rendered virtually impossible. Independent thinking, for example, is not tolerated. Family members must conform to the thinking of the family, to "group think." Or again, family members are expected to follow certain kinds of work or career paths, those paths which conform to the educational level of the family generally. Individual interests (hobbies, sports, music) must comport with and be comprehensible in relation to those shared/required by the family. The choice of a marriage partner must be acceptable. Leaving home, literally or figuratively, is frowned upon, to say the least. Fused families are, in effect, stuck together. And families that are stuck together are, well, stuck; they have difficulty with change, with moving forward.

The same can be said of congregations that are fused. And many are.

Differentiation, then, has to do with how each of us manages being an individual in the midst of the group pressure for togetherness. As individuals, each of us is possessed of differences. Our genuine interests may or may not conform to our family norms. Our thinking may differ, as may our taste in hobbies, sports, and music. The challenge is how to affirm our individuality while at the same time remaining connected to our families of origin. Since initially we depend upon our families for survival, the togetherness force is strong in all of us, and tends to stay strong throughout our lives. The often intense pressure not to affirm our differences, our individuality, our separateness, can also bleed into the way we manage ourselves in any and all groups.

Our maturation, however, requires a lifelong effort at self-definition while at the same time actively sustaining the connection to our families of origin and, by extension, our connection to groups generally. Thus, in the ever changing kaleidoscopic re-patterning of life, differentiation requires the development of a twin capacity to define ourselves as separate persons while at the same time staying connected; it requires the constant management of the tension between togetherness and individuality. The management of this never-entirely-resolvable tension is one of the most challenging of life's tasks.

In any event, differentiation is a process rather than a state of being, a process that can never be fully realized, but can be functionally approximated, with effort. Edwin Friedman, in his book, *The Myth of the Shiksa*, describes self-differentiation as follows (page 158):

Differentiation as used by Bowen [Murray Bowen was the originator of Family Systems theory] refers more to a process than to a goal that can ever be achieved. (When people say, "I differentiated from my wife, my child, my parent, etc.," that proves they do not understand the concept.) It refers to a direction in life rather than a state of being, to the capacity to take a stand in an intense emotional system, to saying "I" when others are demanding "we," to containing one's reactivity to the reactivity of others (which includes the ability to avoid being polarized, to maintaining a non-anxious presence in the face of anxious others). It refers , as well, to knowing where one ends and another begins, to be able to cease automatically being one of the systems dominoes, to being clear about one's own personal values and goals, to taking maximum responsibility for one's own emotional being and destiny rather than blaming others or the context: culture, gender, or environmental forces. It is an emotional concept, not a cerebral one, but it does require clear-headedness. And it has enormous consequences for new ways of thinking about leadership. But it is, as Bowen liked to say, a lifetime project, with no one ever getting more than 70 percent of the way to the goal.

As Friedman's description acknowledges, a self that is more differentiated is less dependent on approval from others, and, concomitantly, less invasive of others. A more differentiated self is a more solid self, is less in need of borrowing self from others. It functions as a less anxious self. To function this way involves a capacity to be able to take "I" positions, to make "I" statements; that is, to actually say what one wants, feels, and believes—which is not the same thing as saying what others should want, feel, believe, or even do. To focus on what others "should" be about is to focus on them, to cede self to others. As much as one might wish that others would "do" differently or be more functional, to "will" them to do differently, aside from making one dependent on the other's compliance, is a kind of fusion (my "self" and some other "self" mush together). The two selves become less differentiated, usually in a dance of willfulness and resistance. A more differentiated self stays focused as non-reactively as possible on what she/he herself/ himself will or won't do, wants or doesn't want.

To further understand differentiation, it can be helpful to examine un-differentiation. (See notes, chapter 3, #2) Less differentiated individuals are highly allergic to ambiguity, are given to black and white, either/or thinking. They focus not on themselves and their own goals, but on others. Indeed, they are obsessed with what's out there and how it may affect (threaten) them. It's an "us against them" mentality. Being empty inside, they want others to fill them up. (And woe unto you if by chance, being a clergy person, you fail to do so.) They panic on a dime. They are super sensitive. They hurt easily, which is a way of making others responsible for their wellbeing. One must walk gingerly around them, which is decidedly controlling on their part. They are connoisseurs of injustice and see themselves as perpetual victims. It (whatever) is always someone else's fault, i.e. they take little or no responsibility for themselves. Self-regulation is beyond them. They are inflexible, dead serious (playfulness being a foreign country), conspiratorial and adept at fomenting secrets. They detest dissent and are totalitarian in outlook. They are polarized and polarizing. A capacity for genuine dialogue is missing.

Un-differentiation is driven by anxiety, by a sense of threat, be it vague or specific. Anxiety is one of the root conditions of being alive. It affects us all, all of the time to some extent, and at some times (times of high stress) to a great extent. During times of high anxiety, the reflexive tendency is to herd or flock together. We have much in common with other animals, being as we are, embedded in nature. In times of high anxiety (marked by fear... fear of most anything—communists, terrorists, anthrax) the fused togetherness force prevails (us and them, right think/wrong think, i.e., "group think" with its polarizing assessment of friends and foes). The real trouble with this panicky state is that it cuts us off from clear thinking, precisely when clear thinking would be most conducive to survival. Under these circumstances, a well differentiated leader who does not succumb to the high reactivity of "group think" may have a beneficial, calming effect, may, by being a less anxious presence, reduce the high level of anxiety/reactivity in the group and help restore a measure of clear-headedness.

This observation is particularly relevant to clergy who must function in leadership positions. To the extent that clergy remain calm in the face of the anxiety/reactivity of their flocks, the more likely it is that the flock itself will calm down and become more clear-headed. This attribute of leadership is not about technique, but rather presence. The more clergy are able to focus on their own functioning (being as non-reactive as possible) rather than on the functioning of the group, the more they may, paradoxically, have a beneficial effect on the overall functioning of the group. This requires a capacity to stand somewhat outside the togetherness force of the group, to retain a measure of objectivity about what is going on.

By way of an aside, it is easy to misconstrue differentiated leadership as some sort of disconnected autonomy, rather like the lone cowboy in the movies, who, having gunned down the bad guys, rides off into the sunset at the end of the film, having barely connected with the people around him, and clearly has no plans to do so in the future. This mythology is not a depiction of genuine differentiation, but rather the depiction of someone who is disconnected from those around him. Emotional connections make him anxious and are completely avoided, implying precisely a chronic lack of differentiation.

In any case, a more differentiated self retains separation from the group (can take "I" positions) while at the same time remaining connected to the various components of the group. An example of a differentiating move occurred in a congregation in which the church drama group decided to mount a production of Tennessee Williams' *Cat on a Hot Tin Roof.* The play, to be performed in the assembly hall, not the sanctuary, was well into rehearsal when the church women's group approached the new pastor, complaining that this was not an appropriate play to be put on by a church sponsored group. The pastor was aware that the women's group and the drama group had a long and ongoing history of conflict. In this installment of the conflict, many in the drama group identified themselves with the characters in "Cat." The women's group regarded the characters as, in no small measure, repulsive.

The women's group asked the new pastor to somehow block the production, which had in fact already been presented to and approved by the governing board prior to the pastor's arrival. This is a classic triangle. As with triangles generally, it tested the pastor's capacity to take a clear stand without simply taking sides.

The pastor's first step was to ask why, having had had an opportunity to object when the choice of play was presented to the governing board, the women's group had failed to do so. He then asked the drama group why they had chosen a play they knew would offend the women's group. These were questions for which the pastor did not require answers. They were asked in a muse-like way, and not in a manner that would put either side on the defensive.

The second step was to give a sermon in the course of which there was a reflection on the play itself. The pastor indicated that he thought *"Cat"* to be a fine play, worthy of production, even in a church. But he also reflected on the characters as being empty, trying to borrow self-worth

31

from each other rather than realizing it to be God-given and already theirs if they could but perceive it. The sermon had the double effect of both appealing to and offending each group. But the most important element was the fact that the pastor took a position of his own without being triangulated into taking sides and without attempting to "fix" the conflict. He managed to differentiate himself by arriving at his own position, focusing on himself and his own functioning, while remaining connected to both groups, which is what differentiation is all about. Incidentally, the minister managed to maintain a good relationship with both groups throughout his long tenure in that place.

Transition as a Time to Focus on Self-differentiation

One way to lower the anxiety that attends most any move to a new position in a new setting is to focus on one's own functioning. The subtext of this statement is that to focus on one's own functioning is to focus as little as possible on the functioning of others. To focus on one's own functioning is a primary way to work on one's own differentiation, which is not to say that the effort to become better differentiated will banish anxiety. It is to say that this effort is key to *managing* anxiety, not only in transitional times, but in life. Here follow some features of what this effort might look like.

32

First, since transitions make things more uncertain, more anxious, rather than less, the understandable tendency is to want to kill the uncertainty, usually by hastening to "get on with it." It's useful to sit with our discomfort and not rush things. The mantra for this period should be "walk, don't run." In systems thinking, the term "non-anxious presence" is often used. But few, if any, are able to be non-anxious in the midst of anxious systems. It is perhaps more accurate to think in terms of being present though anxious.

Second, keep in mind that the next congregation is not the previous congregation. There is a human tendency to try to fit the novelty of the new into the frame of the familiar. Habitual ways of seeing things can skew what's in front of us. Every congregation is different. We should not make up our minds prematurely about what we're experiencing.

Third, share what you think, but share it without requiring agreement. "I statements" are freeing. "We statements" crowd.

Fourth, measure with care what you agree to do. Realize that some parishioners will have to wait until you can get to them. They will survive. This is an exercise in not jumping every time someone says "jump," an initial step in modifying the "pleaser" instinct. Keep what you agree to do within the limits of what time allows given your other commitments to family, to health, to having a life beyond your profession.

Fifth, despite the impingement of those who want you to take responsibility for them and/or the institution, take responsibility only for how you intend to function.

Sixth, work on defining for yourself your core values and where you are going. State these, however partial they may be, whenever appropriate, if for no other reason than to hear yourself say them aloud. Granted, they will continue to evolve. It's a process.

Each of these efforts contributes to the "practice" of becoming more functionally differentiated. The focus of each is on the "being" of the clergy person. It is a focus that can help to reduce susceptibility to the anxiety by which clergy are surrounded.

Chapter Four

Entering a New Field of Anxiety:
The Congregation that Awaits

The congregation into which a newly called, or appointed, clergy person is about to enter is almost certainly as anxious as the clergy person, if not more so. To be sure there is considerable variation in the openness of congregations to the reception of a new pastor. Some congregations will be excited, will be, in effect, disposed to "fall in love," hence the proverbial talk of a honeymoon at the outset. Other congregations will be reticent, perhaps even apprehensive (not much given to a honeymoon). Some will be easier to read, others more difficult; some readily accepting, others highly guarded.

All blessings on those entering receptive, energized, highly functional settings. In my experience, and from what I've gleaned from colleagues over the years, such settings are rare. Many, if not most clergy must deal initially with less than optimal conditions. In this context, "less than optimal" means that the level of anxiety in the congregation is high, if not through the ceiling. The particulars of high anxiety in a congregation usually have to do with how the disengagement from the previous ministry was managed. As noted in chapter one, unresolved emotional intensities have a life of their own. When clergy enter a new congregation, they walk smack into them.

Four Examples of Highly Anxious Congregational Behavior

1. Upon visiting the congregation to which he was about to move, a minister was immediately accosted by a small group of his soon-to-be parishioners about how badly the previous minister had been treated and ultimately dispatched. They were outraged at the lay leadership for letting the malcontents in the congregation have their way. They wanted the new pastor to feel their hurt and to become their ally against a morally deficient leadership (their fellow congregants). Their collective rant went on for a full hour and was only terminated by the fact that the pastor was overdue for a meeting with the church leadership. That he was going off to meet with the leadership only fueled the group's aggrieved sense of their being left out, of not being heard. They feared that the new minister would be "taken over" by "the terrible leadership."

In systems thinking, this is an instance of triangulation. The aggrieved group wanted the new minister to join them against the offending leadership. The leadership, for their part, wanted the minister to ally himself with them against their detractors. The suck on the minister to take sides was intense. The challenge for the minister was to maintain a straight, open relationship with both parties without emotionally allying himself with either, emotionally, even if he statedly agreed with one side more than the other. In any event, anxiety in this congregation manifested itself as polarization.

2. A young woman just starting out in her ministry and needing to start somewhere accepted a call (though with misgivings) to a church which had long been losing members and was decidedly short on funds. The worry was that if things didn't turn around, the church would have to close its doors. The congregation was looking to her, as she was told repeatedly, to reverse the decline in membership, to grow the church, at which task the previous minster, though very nice, had been woefully inadequate. The unspoken dimension of this call was that if she failed to deliver the needed growth, like the previous minister, the fault would

be hers, not theirs. Anxiety, in this instance, manifested itself as congregational under-functioning, that is, as a not-so-subtle demand that the pastor over-function for them.

3. The previous minister, an alcoholic, was fired after exhaustive efforts on the part of the congregation's leadership to provide the needed rehabilitation. Not surprisingly, the congregation was polarized over the termination, as he'd been for many an effective pastor. The congregation was further polarized, however, by the fact that he had been a strong advocate and activist for social justice, taking positions in the pulpit that went down well with the more liberal members, but with the more conservative members resulted in something akin to heartburn. All of these factors resulted in multiple, sometimes overlapping polarizations; e.g., a conservative man who didn't care for the minister's theological politics was nonetheless deeply appreciative of his ministry at the time of his wife's death, while a woman who could not tolerate alcoholism (having grown up in an alcoholic family) identified with the minister's liberal positions. These two persons could have ended up on either end of the spectrum—wanting either his termination or his retention, but each for

quite contradictory reasons. Upon arrival, the new minister was faced with a bewildering jungle of polarizations, difficult to get a handle on, much less sort out. The fractured membership attempted to enlist his sympathy and support in multiple directions—to claim him as the confidant of some, not others. Indeed, if at coffee hour after Sunday worship the new minister was seen even so much as talking to some members, other members would be miffed.

Here again there was triangulation, but, in this instance, the scene was laced with many interlocking triangles—an even more difficult condition with which to cope. The anxiety in this congregation manifested itself in many highly layered, unpredictable polarizations. (See notes, chapter 4, #1)

4. A new minister arrived at a congregation that had experienced the sudden departure of its previous minister, about which little was actually said. For some indefinable reason, the conversations felt repressed. The energy level was low, the connections between congregants distant. It didn't take long for the new minister to realize that the church was full of gossip and secrets. Communication on all levels was dismal. Even

arranging for the use and set-up of the community room was a tragic-comedy of mishaps. Nothing was easily accomplished. Organizational dysfunction was rampant. The new minister finally ascertained that the previous minister had been acting out sexually, but that no one wanted to speak of it. Anxiety can take the form of volatile polarity at one end, or, as in this case, de-energized repression at the other.

All of these depictions of anxiety fall at the higher end of the scale. Regrettably these scenarios are not unusual or rare. Whatever field of anxiety a clergy person may have left (with which there was at least the comfort of familiarity), the new one is precisely that—*new*; the anxiety landscape is unfamiliar and inevitably "ups" the clergy person's anxiety. And this becomes the issue: how does one manage one's own "upped" anxiety? For anxiety is contagious. It flows through systems, be those systems churches, schools, small business, huge corporations, or governments.

As the incoming leader, a new clergy person is in the vortex of the institutional anxiety flow. It comes right at and encompasses her/him. That flow, whether intense or moderate, usually pressures the newly arriving clergy person to fix something—probably lots of "somethings." And, more often than not, the clergy person sets about being the "fixer," attempting to competently deliver what's being asked. What is often overlooked, however, is that "the fix" in-coming clergy have been "called" by the congregation to implement will frequently be resisted; the very "improvements" clergy feel mandated to provide will, to the clergy's bewilderment, often be sabotaged. Why? Because most "fixes" involve change. Change may be desired theoretically, but is often highly threatening when actually implemented.

For example, congregations with declining membership, anxious for survival, often call new clergy leadership to "grow the church." Necessarily, growth means change. Indeed, even before new members show up, changes are likely to be required in order for the church to attract new members; changes, whether they be a different musical style and/or programs that appeal to a growing ethnic population in the immediate neighborhood, are not always welcome. Such changes, though essential if the church is to grow, are likely to be resisted. Thus, paradoxically, anxiety cuts both ways, simultaneously asking for change and, in what can feel to clergy like perversity, sabotaging it. Anxiety drives both the proclaimed desire for change and the resistant sabotage.

How can this seeming "paradox," this wish for yet resistance to change, be explained? It has to do with institutional homeostasis, an unappreciated reality not only in churches, but in institutions generally. Homeostasis is the interior balance of relationships that structure group stability. Homeostasis is also an anxiety binder. In its capacity to bind anxiety and promote stability, however, homeostasis is remarkably effective in warding off change. The difficulty is that there are times when change is more essential to survival than stability. The group's anxious resistance to change, its homeostasis, can have the unintended consequence of doing the group in. There are times when groups, for their own good, need to tolerate less homeostasis and more anxiety.

In any event, resistance to change that has been officially mandated can put clergy in an awkward position at best, a no win situation at worst. To be sure, some congregants will resist more than others, and within a given congregation the resistance may be minority driven. But minorities are often in control. Though some congregations are ready and willing to run with a new minister, given the likely presence of resistance, clergy do well not to fall too quickly into the role of Reverend Fixit. When responsibility for change is handed to the incoming minister, a little nonplused helplessness can go a long way toward returning responsibility to those to whom it actually belongs.

Clergy often feel obliged to have "the answers." Over-functioning is something of a professional liability. Clergy can be far more empowering of their parishioners if they hold off knowing it all, doing it all, if they raise more questions than they proffer answers, if they don't do for parishioners what parishioners can and should do for themselves. Admittedly, this holding back goes against the grain of a normal desire to demonstrate capability and competence. It is counter-intuitive. Nonetheless, not knowing it all and doing it all, a touch of helplessness, can cut down the subtle and sometimes not-so-subtle resistance to change. This alone can be for clergy a great stress reducer.

In any event, the inclination of clergy to please (i.e. over-function) easily turns them into waste disposal stations for the content of the congregation's anxiety. It is essential that clergy reduce stress (and enhance health) by shifting the anxiety that will most assuredly be dumped on them back into the system. "Have you spoken with the building committee members about what you've told me of your objection to spending so much on new carpet in the sanctuary? No? Can you speak to them? You don't think you can? Why not? If I go with you, would that help? No? I could, on your behalf, though I'd rather you did it yourself, convey your concerns to the committee, inviting them to speak with you directly about them. Let you be anonymous? No, that I can't do. You see, [taking a stand around clear values] I believe parish concerns/complaints need to be conveyed directly, and not anonymously, to the proper church officials. I would be glad to help you do that, but am not willing to do that for you and leave you out of it." For carpet concerns one can substitute here concerns about the music program, or objections to the church's financial support of its denomination, given objectionable positions the denomination has taken, etc.

For clergy and congregational health alike, it is essential that clergy be as calmly, non-reactively unreceptive to this dumping as possible. The challenge then is how not to be drawn into the anxiety of the system, is how to be a non-anxious (or at least less anxious) presence in a not non-anxious system, especially in times of transition.

Chapter Five

Seven Questions for Managing One's Own Anxiety Upon Entering the Congregation that Awaits

Clergy can be and often are accosted by parishioners with intense, sometimes angry agendas at coffee hour, in the church parking lot, before and after meetings, via late evening phone calls, often when they're least expecting it. Clergy who have been in place for some time, who know the people, are in a better position than newly arrived clergy to read whatever is coming at them, which may enable them to remain calm. But even for pastors who have been in place for awhile, remaining non-reactive to reactivity can be a challenge. For newly arrived clergy, it's likely to be even harder.

Not unlike therapists dealing with volatile clients, clergy in new situations can make use of questions that may disarm confrontational reactivity. Good questions can help clergy feel less besieged, indeed *be* less besieged, by nudging parishioners toward a less reactive mode of functioning. Questions can also help clergy manage their own reactivity to the reactivity coming at them. Here are seven

45

multilayered questions that may prove useful. (See notes, chapter 5, #1)

Question area #1:
Dealing with Embitterment

A member corners the new minister at coffee hour with an embittered tirade about the lay leadership for their unconscionable treatment of the former minister. (This is similar to the first example in chapter four.) He wants the new minister to become an ally against a mendacious leadership. The implication clearly enough is that if the new minister doesn't become an ally, the aggrieved member will contemplate leaving the church, which just as clearly will be accounted the new minster's fault. (Triangulation is a primary container and perpetrator of anxiety.)

A potentially useful question in this circumstance would be: *"What was the hardest thing for you when Rev. So-and-so left?"*

This may shift the focus from misdirected anger to the member's own genuine grief over losing a pastor to whom he has been very attached. Or it may not. It does, however, shift the focus away from what the new minister is being pressured to do for "the complainant" to how the member is or is not handling his own "aggrievement."

As an aside, this question is also useful in helping those who are not embittered, but who are attempting to process the loss of the former pastor.

Other similar questions might include: *"How has the leave-taking affected you?" "Did a part of you depart when Rev. So-and-so departed?" "What are you doing to resolve this for yourself?" "Do you think you'll ever be able to get over it?"* Again, this puts the focus on what the member might or might not be able to do to manage himself. It also sidesteps the parishioner's manipulative desire to be dependent upon a minister, any minster, for his wellbeing.

The minister can go even further in this direction: *"I can see how hurt you are. It must be taking a heavy toll. How do you find the strength to continue as a member here? I'm not sure I could bring myself to stay if I felt as you do."*

In posing this question, the new minister is refusing to be hostage to the disgruntled parishioner's threat to leave. The minister "goes the other way;" that is, he pushes the member and his threat to leave together rather than trying to pull them apart. Whether this approach arouses resistance (resistance to leaving) remains to be seen, but it functions to keep the minister from serving as a ready receptacle for systemic anxiety.

Question area #2:
Dealing with the Past Recycled

A congregation has become polarized over whether to build a new sanctuary. The differences over the need for a new sanctuary and "losing" the old one have become acrimonious, opinion being evenly divided. Both factions want the new minister to see things their way and there is intense pressure for her to take a stand. At this early junction the minister lacks a leaning either way, but the conflict threatens to split the congregation. Both sides accost her often and vociferously to take one side against the other. The general behavior is nasty and intractable.

In these circumstances, she might, each time she is engaged by various members on both sides of the debate, begin to ask repeatedly, *"In your memory has there ever been as divisive a controversy as this?"* (Chances are exceptionally good that there have been.) *"Tell me about it."*

Or again, *"How in the world do you account for the way people are thinking about this issue?"* *"Is there any point made by the other side that makes sense to you?"*

Perhaps there have been controversies in the more distant past. These things can and do recycle. Looking at the history of the church, often ignored, is highly useful. For example, did it begin by splitting off from a "mother" church over some disagreement?

One question that puts the responsibility squarely back on the members is, *"If this congregation splits over this issue, how long do you think it will be before we'll have to close our doors?"* Also, *"Do you think I should begin circulating my resume?"*

Here again, the minister "stiff-arms" anxiety by refusing to be a receptacle for it, by placing it back into the system where it belongs.

Question area #3:
Dealing with Misplaced Expectations

Unlike area #2, and in contrast to high intensity conflict, some congregations go through periods of low morale. There may be complaints that things just aren't what they used to be. Fond memories are regularly recalled of halcyon days, of an overflowing church school and packed pews on Sunday mornings. It's a common lament in not a few mainline churches.

A new minister may feel charged, however subtly, with the task of pumping up the congregation's heart rate, in effect, with recovering the congregation's youth. Here again, pushing the responsibility back into the system is appropriate.

Useful questions include the following: *"When was it good here?" "What would it take for things to be good again now?" "What specific steps could we take?" "How could you help us take those steps?"*

A question designed to redirect the focus from chronic complaint to recognizing current strengths could also be employed: *"Is there anything about the church the way it is now that you'd hate to lose?"*

Inviting congregants to identify their own strengths is likely to be more productive than trying to be a super-clergy person supplying what's missing (which obliquely imputes weakness to the congregation).

Question area #4:
Dealing with Unresolved Pain

The previous minister has run off with the church organist. To keep this from being totally stereotypical, let's make it a female minister that has run off with a male organist. Or pick any betrayal that embarrasses a congregation.

The newly arrived minister is following a duplicity that has severely undermined trust. Projections fly, lighting easily on the new clergy person. The unspoken question is: "Will you betray and embarrass us, too?"

When possible, ask congregants questions such as: *"What did Rev. So-and-so and organist So-and-so's behavior and sudden departure bring up for you?" "What has been the hardest thing about it?" "If the opportunity arose, what would you like to say to each of them?" "How do you think they (either of them) would respond?"*

The goal is to push parishioners toward the sources of their pain, rather than merely commiserating with them about it, thereby inviting them to deal more directly and perhaps more maturely with their afflictions. This prevents the clergy person from carrying more of the system's anxiety than necessary.

Question area #5:
Dealing with Secrets

Some congregations are hives of secrets. A major secret usually engenders secretive behavior throughout a congregation. Secretiveness, in turn, engenders gossip. It is a systemic phenomenon.

An alcoholic Senior Minister at a multi-staffed church (similar to case three in chapter four) was adept at keeping his habit concealed from most in the congregation. The other clergy on staff were aware of the Senior Minister's "problem," as were the non-clergy administrative staff. It happened that the principle administrative assistant was also an alcoholic. Sympathetically, she covered for him as much as possible, in effect colluding in the concealment.

Slowly, the unacknowledged "problem" became evident to members of the congregation. There was "talk"—that is, gossip. Eventually the Senior Minister's condition was too self-evident to be concealed or denied. After repeated offers to undergo rehab programs, all refused, he was terminated. The new minister found himself in an ongoing pattern of secretive behavior, in a sea of gossip, even though the alcoholic minister was no longer around.

The very nature of secretive gossip is to talk to one so-and-so about another, non-present so-and-so. When approached with this kind of talk, the minister might well ask, *"Have you spoken directly with 'the other' so-and so about this?"* (The gossiper usually hasn't.) *"If I accompanied you, could you do it then?"* (Usually not.) *"Would you like me to pass along what you've said about 'the other' so-and-so, indicating of course that you've said it?"* (Usually the last thing the gossiper wants.) *"I'm happy to do so; in fact, if you won't, I think it important that I do."* This is a gossip killer. "Outing" secretive behavior almost always squelches it.

The minister can also respond to the pervasiveness of gossip by repeating it aloud in small groups, asking in a simple-minded sort of way, *"Why do you suppose people are saying what they're saying?"*

When that famous line, "people are saying," is dumped on the minster, the minister does well to ask for names, because she/he considers it absolutely essential to talk directly to "them" (whoever they are) about "whatever." Usually, when specific names are asked for, the identities of "the people who are saying" suddenly evaporate. Keep asking for them.

When a minister hears that someone is in fact talking about her/him in a complaining mode (it happens), it is wise/useful to go directly to the person, ascertain the accuracy of what has been heard, respond as pastorally as possible, but also, in the course of conversation, stress a personal preference that complaints or negative commentary about the clergy person be addressed to her/him directly.

Question area #6:
Dealing with Weak Leadership

The newly arrived female Associate Minister of a large church led by an emotionally remote Senior Minister was assigned the supervisory responsibility for the lay leader of the youth program, a male in his early twenties. As it happened, the youth leader's father was the chairperson of the governing board of the church. It became evident to the Associate that the young man had questionably appropriate relationships with some of the female participants, being overly physically familiar with certain of them at the edges of the meetings. When, in a supervisory session, she spoke to him about his behavior, being clear that it must stop, he threatened that his father would see to it that she would be fired. The Senior Minister, himself intimidated by this lay leader, when told by the Associate about the threat, directed her to drop the entire matter.

After giving it considerable thought, she came to the conclusion that any untoward fallout from the young man's behavior would rebound to what would be regarded as her inadequate supervision and that she would likely be fired. Dropping the matter, besides being against her principles, was not, she decided, a real option.

She requested from the Senior Minister a letter of recommendation, explaining that when the lawsuits arrived, she wished to be off staff. She added, *"In your opinion, how best might I explain to the congregation my reasons for leaving?"* (Indicating that she would certainly credit him with the reasoning in her letter of resignation.)

The Senior Minister decided he ought to take the matter up with the father/board chairperson, who, as it happened, was a lawyer. Lawsuits this man understood. The youth leader suddenly resigned. The Associate's position remained secure.

In this instance, the Associate placed the problem/anxiety where it belonged, with the Senior Minister. Passive leadership at the top invariably poses difficulties for those working just below. Being prepared to say to such a "leader," one way or another, "how would you like me to explain to the congregation the reasons for my resignation," may challenge the passivity. Or it may not. It is a high-risk position to adopt. Being prepared to actually resign in such situations is a prerequisite.

A less high-stakes question would be, *"Given the circumstances in which I find myself powerless to correct the questionable behavior of the youth leader, I don't think I can continue in my present supervisory role. Is there another role on this church staff for which I am better suited?"*

Question area #7:
Dealing with Under-and Over-functioning

New ministers often arrive with ideas, some of them possibly innovative, about programs that could or should be implemented, about things that could or should be fixed, about where the congregation could or should be headed. The issue is getting the congregation to buy in. Granted some congregations are possessed of vitality and energy and don't require extra motivation. But not many. More frequently the minister finds her or himself "willing" the congregation to change its reluctant, even somnolent ways. The underlying reality is, however, the more clergy "will" congregations to change, or merely to get up off their duffs and do something, the more likely congregations are to "sit tight," the more likely clergy will be resisted. Generally, a congregation's resistance takes the form of under-functioning. But it may also take the form of overt conflict, of a direct "no, we won't!"

In the over/under functioning dance, a more balanced relationship is most likely to be achieved when over-functioning clergy "defect in place," that, is, when they stay connected to the congregation, remain very present, not distant, but don't do for the congregation what it could and should do for itself. To defect in place, it is crucial for clergy not to allow their wellbeing to become dependent on the functioning of others—in this case on the functioning of the congregation. One element in realizing this non-dependence is for clergy to have personal goals that are independent of their professional life, that are not bound up with the functioning or non-functioning of the congregation. In other words, they need to have a life… a life apart from their professional life. It's almost mystical, but as soon as clergy make space not to be thinking about their congregants *all the time*, their congregants know it and will start moving toward their leader rather than away, and concomitantly resistance will likely subside, at least somewhat.

In any event, given the propensity of clergy to over-function (admittedly a generalization, not universally true), the questions to ask in this area are best addressed to oneself. They include:

"From whom in my family did I learn to pick up the ball when others drop it?" "Is there a generational pattern of over-functioners matched with under-functioners in my family of origin?" "Am I the oldest sibling in my family?" "If so, do I have to be an oldest sibling for everybody?" "Who is in control when I over-function for an under-functioner?" (Answer: the under-functioner.) *"Am I dependent on others being dependent (seemingly) on me?" "Is it really true that if only I tried harder, everything would be okay?" "Has it ever come true that everything has been okay (the Kingdom has been realized) because I tried harder?" "Why am I so*

tired?" (Answer: because doing for others what others should be doing for themselves is both draining and stressful.)

It must be understood that the questions within each of these seven subject areas arise not out of a technique to be memorized, but from a practice—dare I say a spiritual practice—that takes unrelenting discipline. Reactivity (not reacting to reactivity) is rarely mastered completely. Differentiation, as Bowen insisted, is never more than 70% realized and, for the vast majority of us, is nowhere near that.

Furthermore, these questions are by no means an exhaustive list. They are samples of how clergy may be able to exercise a measure of control over their own reactivity. They are conceptual tools for self-management. They are not prescriptive. No label accompanies them with the words: "use as directed." Rather, the implicit hope here is that clergy will come up with their versions, fitted to their own circumstances.

Chapter Six

Summing Up

It is a life-long challenge for any of us, clergy or not, to comport ourselves as non-anxious presences, or at least less-anxious presences. For clergy, the challenge is compounded when they undertake a transition from one congregation to another. The challenge begins when they contemplate a move, when they begin their search for a new congregational partner. The effort of both clergy and congregations is to discern if they are a match. It is assumed that the ingredients of a good match have to do with compatibility, with sharing similar outlooks and tastes. What usually goes unnoticed is that how well the partners in a new clergy/congregational marriage will bond has less to do with their compatibility and more to do with how each managed the disengagement from their previous relationships. It is therefore of inestimable value that both clergy and congregations disengage well. The leave-taking is best if it is not hurried, if time is taken to properly honor the time spent together.

Leave-taking is part of a transition. Entering is the other part. Sometimes the leaving and entering partially overlap so that the demands on clergy come from both ends of the transition process. This makes it crucial that clergy focus on their own functioning, on what they wish to be about, on self-definition, on what they will and will not respond to, this in contrast to focusing on what others (possibly two congregations at once) may be demanding.

Clergy are often over-functioners. Times of transition invite clergy to over-function even more than usual. Indeed, the demands on them may virtually double during transitional times, which is why it becomes essential for clergy to use the transitional time to focus on how they will, and will not, function.

At the start, almost every new situation is awash in anxiety. Upon arrival, clergy can become collecting rods for the high voltage content of the congregations' reactivity to change. It is therefore essential that clergy find ways of managing their own reactivity to the congregation's reactivity. They must begin with themselves. Self-management is key to lowering anxiety in the system. This is a new concept for leadership, that it focus not on strategies for manipulating the system, but rather on one's self. The effort in self-management is to function as a non-anxious (or less anxious) presence. To function as a less-anxious presence does not mean one is anxiety free. It means that one is functioning less anxiously despite the discomfort of one's own inescapable anxiety.

To this end, the previous chapter offered seven questions (or areas of disarming inquiry) designed to assist clergy in managing their own anxiety as they enter a new setting. Though it may not be self-evident, the questions themselves are aimed less at lowering anxiety in confrontational congregants and/or situations than at lowering the clergy's own anxiety. But the powerful effect of lowering anxiety in the congregation's leader can be a lowering of anxiety in the system, that is, in the congregation. Lower anxiety results in higher functioning.

To repeat what I said in the introduction, this monograph is over-full of advice. Advice-giving, I readily admit, is largely ineffective. Nonetheless, chapter 2 elucidated what I count as good advice when leaving a congregation. But again, I must emphasize that I wish I'd thought to do even half of what that chapter suggests when I was in the process of disengaging from my various pastorates. I wish I'd had at tongue-tip even some of the questions cited in Chapter 5 when negotiating my own transitions between calls. I didn't. But they are offered, as is this short book, in the hope that the thinking will be of use to others in managing themselves in the midst of negotiating the rapids of a "white water ministry."

Notes

Chapter One

1. The examples cited throughout are based on actual events/circumstances, but the content is significantly altered in order not to reference specific persons or situations.

2. I am explicitly indebted to Edwin Friedman's thinking for the essential premise of this book; namely that how well people engage with each other has less to do with compatibility than how they disengage from previous associations. It is his view that engagement and disengagement are inextricably entwined, that how healthily new relationships may evolve has more to do with the carryover of unresolved emotional intensity from previous relationships than with what people think they have in common. Friedman spells this out as a contributor (chapter 10) in the book *Practicing Family Therapy in Diverse Settings*, Jossey Bass Social and Behavioral Science, Jossey-Bass

publishers, 1984. Friedman's chapter is titled, *A Family Approach to Pre-Marital Counseling.* It is his contention that how well pre-marital couples manage to disengage from their families of origin, while still staying connected, has more impact on how well they bond with each other than does their presumed compatibility. He further contends that this same principle applies to clergy as they separate from former congregations and bond with new ones.

Chapter Two

1. It is debatable as to whether some steps toward undertaking the search might take place during the leave-taking time. The point still holds: the primary focus should be on saying goodbye rather than on mounting a new search, even if elements of the search are to be undertaken during this time.

Chapter Three

1. I am indebted to Peter Steinke for this one-liner.
2. I am indebted to Edwin Friedman for these descriptors of un-differentiation, many of which are contained in a handout titled *Twelve Characteristics of the Undifferentiated Parishioner*, as well as various other places in his writings.

Chapter Four

1. It is well to keep in mind that emotionally polarized congregations are likely displacing anxieties that arise in the homes of the members. Much congregational conflict is less about its purported content than it is rooted in conflict in the congregation's many families.

Chapter Five

1. The impetus for this chapter, indeed, for this book, arose from a clergy systems group, in which one of the members who was about to move to a new church appointment asked me to come up with seven questions to help him parry the exceedingly high anxiety that was already assaulting him from the new setting. "That's an interesting assignment," I quipped. When I got home, I thought, "That *is* an interesting assignment." The questions I subsequently sent him seemed to help, or so he reported.

Bibliography for Further Reading

Bowen, Murray. 1978. *Family Therapy in Clinical Practice*. New York: Jason Aronson

Friedman, Edwin H. 1985. *Generation to Generation: Family Process in church and Synagogue*. New York: Guilford Press.

Friedman, Edwin H. 2007. *A Failure of Nerve: Leadership in the Age of the Quick Fix*. Seabury Books.

Friedman, Edwin H. 2008. *Myth of the Shiksa and Other Essays*. New York: Church Publishing.

Gilbert, Roberta. 1992. *Extraordinary Relationships: A New Way of Thinking About Human Interactions*. New York: John Wiley and Sons.

Kerr, Michael E. Kerr and Bowen, Murray. 1988. *Family Evaluation : The Role of the Family as an Emotional Unit That Governs Individual Behavior and Development*, New York: Norton.

McGoldrick, Monica and Gerish, Randy, 1985. *Genograms in Family Assessment*. W.W. Norton.

Richardson, Ronald W. 1984. *Family Ties That Bind*: *A Self-Help Guide to Change through Family of Origin Therapy*. Vancouver: Self-Counsel Press.

Richardson, Ronald W. 1996. *Creating a Healthier Church*. Fortress Press.

Titelman, Peter, Editor, 2003. *Emotional Cutoff: Bowen Family Systems Theory Perspectives*, The Haworth Clinical Practice Press.

Rev. Phillip Washburn served the Scarsdale Congregational Church (United Church of Christ) in Scarsdale, New York, as Senior Minister for twenty-four years until his retirement. Prior to Scarsdale he served churches in Dumfries, Scotland; Chapel Hill, North Carolina; and Hamden, Connecticut. He studied Family Systems thinking with Dr. Edwin Friedman (author of Generation to Generation and A Failure of Nerve) for seven years and has since conducted workshops in church settings, for judicatory staff, and clergy retreats. He has also worked with a variety of small clergy groups focusing on coping with difficulties in parish settings from a Systems perspective. He now resides in Chapel Hill, North Carolina.

CPSIA information can be obtained at www.ICGtesting.com
Printed in the USA
LVOW081923130912

298705LV00002B/112/P